Finding Satisfaction Within
By: Tanya
Co-Authored By:
Jill M. Brown
Version 2.0 – November 2020
Published by Tanya
Copyright © 2020 by Tanya
All rights reserved, including the right of reproduction in whole or in part in any form.

My Journey…

The visions began when I was seven. It was the first day of school and I remember the chaos of children in the classroom. It was not until my classmates became quiet, did I realize I was seeing and hearing things that were not physically happening in the classroom. The imagery was blurry; much like the vision of a person not wearing prescription glasses. Nothing was taking focus. Additionally, it sounded like a large roomful of people whispering around me. I remember feeling very frightened and panicky. And then I fainted.

When I awoke, my parents were beside me and I was taken home. To calm my 7-year-old psyche, tea, cookies, and cartoons were administered for the remainder of the day. Rightfully concerned about my emotional wellbeing, my parents called in reinforcements. My next memory is of my maternal grandmother entering my bedroom. While lying in bed, I could smell burning sage. Crystals were then placed at the top of my head, forehead, ears, and throat, continuing down my body. While these crystals were in place, my grandmother began to verbally pray. Some of the words she used while praying scared me and so she began to string the words together into songs.

The singing calmed me. I was completely unaware of what was really transpiring. The prayers were shutting down my 3rd eye chakra so that I would stop having visions.

The 3rd eye chakra is connected to the brain, and my ability to learn effectively was also being shut down. It would be years before I would come to understand these actions and the connected ramifications.

Afterward, life resumed. I attended school but it became exceedingly difficult to learn to read and write. Conceptual understanding and memory also became troublesome. The world, as I knew it, was hazy. I was not functioning normally, and subsequently spent a lot of my time in front of the tv. My childhood continued this way and it continued without grandma.

Then there were the dreams. I started receiving signals in my sleep, but I did not understand that at the time. Before long, I noticed these dreams coming to life, exactly as dreamt, in real time. I was intrigued but not afraid - probably because the material was neither freaky nor tragic. These nightly occurrences did cause me to question my mother. I repeatedly asked about what it all meant, and her common response was to tell me to 'brush it off,' that it was nothing abnormal.

I had no knowledge of metaphysical gifts on the maternal side of my family. I had no idea that my grandmother's talents also flowed through my mother. I had no idea how difficult their lives had been before me. I did not know that communities lashed out at their abilities with weapons of fear and hatred, spitting 'witch' in their faces. My mother's unconventional upbringing left her ignoring her talent, and it also left her protecting her daughter from societal prejudices. She worked extremely hard at being "normal", so it is no surprise she feared grandmother shedding light on my spiritual abilities. My parents kept her away from me for 5 years.

My father passed when I was 12. A long-term battle of diabetes ended his life on earth, but after his passing, it became obvious death had not ended his presence in my life. He began visiting me in dreams. I voiced these first few visitations to my mother. She tried to comfort me by explaining that my dad was now an angel and he was watching over me. According to my mom, my dreams were normal and natural.

The visitations went from occasional to nightly. Instead of just appearing in my dreams, he began to speak. Initially he spoke in fragments: "I'm sorry" and "I did this." Confused, I began to write down everything I saw and heard during these visitations. The fragments evolved into sentences. One night he clearly said, "I'm sorry I closed you down." When I responded with confusion, the following night his message was "I'm sorry I took your gift away." At this point I demanded an explanation from my mother. Eventually she yielded by having my grandmother return to explain all that had been hidden from me.

Grandma revealed everything. She explained my psychic and medium capabilities. To say I was stunned would be a gross understatement. I was very frightened. It took days for me to not only digest this information, but to calm down. After much conversation (and more singing), my grandmother gradually soothed me enough so that the shaking and hyperventilating ended. Grandma stayed with me and life seemed to normalize in her presence.

I was then given a life choice at the wise age of 12. I could either continue living with my mother or I could move to be with grandma. If I chose to move, the understanding was that my 3rd eye would be reopened, allowing the visions to return. It really did not take long for me to decide. I opted for a clearer life and soon found myself moving two states west of my mother.

As my mental block was lifting, life started to become gloriously clear. I was happier with this newfound clarity of thought. Little by little my reading improved. I felt better. It was a new world, and I was seeing it through fresh eyes. For the first time there was potential for learning with the probability of a future – a future, free of haze.

The next 8 years my world consisted of training. My grandmother taught me how to read signs, both spiritual and physical. I was trained to understand the art of listening to spirit guides and angels. Communicating with spirits, blocking negativity, and protecting oneself from spiritual attacks were fundamental to my education. I was taught rituals and lessons that had been passed down through my family's generations. I learned how crystals and essential oils can heal the spirit. I was also instructed on the art of closing doors on past lives. At the age of 20 my resume' included psychic, medium, healer, energy specialist, tarot card reader, palm reader and un-locker of past lives. It was this knowledge that led me to begin a life of helping and healing.

If you have ever wondered about your purpose in life or who you are meant to be with, you believe in something greater than yourself. The belief that there is something more divine is a belief in God. If you are more comfortable referring to the divine as the Universe, I am including that description here as well.

    For the last 20 years, I have been able to assist many people in my practice, but this book enables me to reach individuals I could never meet in person. My hope is to provide people with specific tools to finding true happiness. With a little knowledge and a willingness to explore a new path, you can absolutely achieve satisfaction within. So, open your heart and mind, have faith, and watch the beauty that is about to unfold.

Chapter 1: New Beginnings, The Crown Chakra & Peace

It seems to me that a large percentage of our society does not know how to be 'whole' anymore. My clients convey what they believe to be lacking in their lives. Whether that is wanting to find true love or change career paths, people are commonly unhappy in one or more areas. In general, people want the same thing - to be satisfied. We want to be satisfied with ourselves, our jobs, our marriages, and with our families. We are all striving for satisfaction.

Every individual is aware of their physical bodies, but what might be news to many is that we also possess a spiritual body (more on that in the next chapter). When those two bodies are in harmony, we feel satisfied. When they are not in harmony, spiritual and physical discord take place. Just as our bodies need exercise for good health, our spirit bodies need the same. To avoid disharmony, our spiritual bodies need strengthening.

Regaining harmony between the physical and the spiritual does not require much in the way of time or money. In fact, a great deal of change can take place within days. But, before the recipe, I want to first explain and illustrate some fundamentals, as well as give examples of significant life changes that have occurred within my clients' worlds.

UNSATISFIED = OUT OF ALIGNMENT

SATISFIED = IN ALIGNMENT

Peace and the Crown Chakra…

Carl is in the passenger seat of the car as his mother drives them around town. They are happily shopping for his upcoming year of college. While talking, they fail to notice the oncoming vehicle in their lane. The cars collide horribly. Carl suffers a concussion from the crash, but it is fatal for his mother. He watches in horror as she slips away. He is 19 and his life has been instantly transformed.

Years later, Carl is my very first client. He requests a telephone reading because he cannot bring himself to physically leave his house. Tethered by landlines, we begin to work together.

His primary fear is death. This makes sense to me after knowing the details of the car accident. Even over the phone, Carl's fear is palpable. He is struggling with several phobias and does not realize how he has normalized them. His spiritual body and physical body are in disharmony. The problems do not stop there; Carl has also developed a stutter.

Apart from wanting to shed his phobias, Carl wants someone to love. I agree to assist him, but I explain that due to his disharmonious state, he needs to be on his life path. Using a metaphor, I ask him to envision people who are on their life paths as people driving cars on a highway. The goal here is to be driving, not walking – Carl was walking. He was not up to speed (so to speak) - spiritually he was stuck. To be driving, healing, and strengthening of the crown chakra had to take place. I prescribed mental exercises to begin the process.

I had Carl visualize the life he wanted. This included walking out his front door, riding a bike and imagining the kind of life he would have with a future love. He diligently worked on the visualizations. Small victories led to larger victories, and he began to manifest a sense of power. His confidence continued to grow.

Through meditation and with the aid of crystals and essential oils (more on this in chapters 3 &4), the mind-body-spirit connection eventually became balanced. After being completely housebound for 13 years, Carl was able to walk outside. Not only did he have the power to leave the confines of his home, but he was also smiling, laughing, and sleeping well. The stutter disappeared. He shed his fear and attained his goals. It did not take long before he landed a job. While working, he found the woman of his dreams. Finally, Carl was able to find happiness and satisfaction through his peace and through his crown.

Chapter 2: Energy Centers, The 3rd Eye Chakra & Wealth

Our spiritual body is made up of chakras. Chakras are energy centers that basically govern our psychological qualities. The human body has hundreds of chakras, but our focus will be on the main 7. Our upper body houses 4 chakras that govern mental properties, while our lower body includes 3 chakras that control our instinctive properties.

Commonly the 7 main chakras are listed in order, beginning from the bottom with the root chakra listed as #1. We are reversing the order here and beginning at what I believe to be the beginning, the crown chakra. God/Universe are above us, and since our crown chakra is a direct pathway to God/Universe, the crown chakra is #1.

I like to think of the top 3 chakras as God/Universe. They represent our connection to God/Universe, the mind, and the voice. The heart chakra stands alone like the sun, bright and strong. The bottom 3 chakras, representing our grounding, power, and core—are the earth.

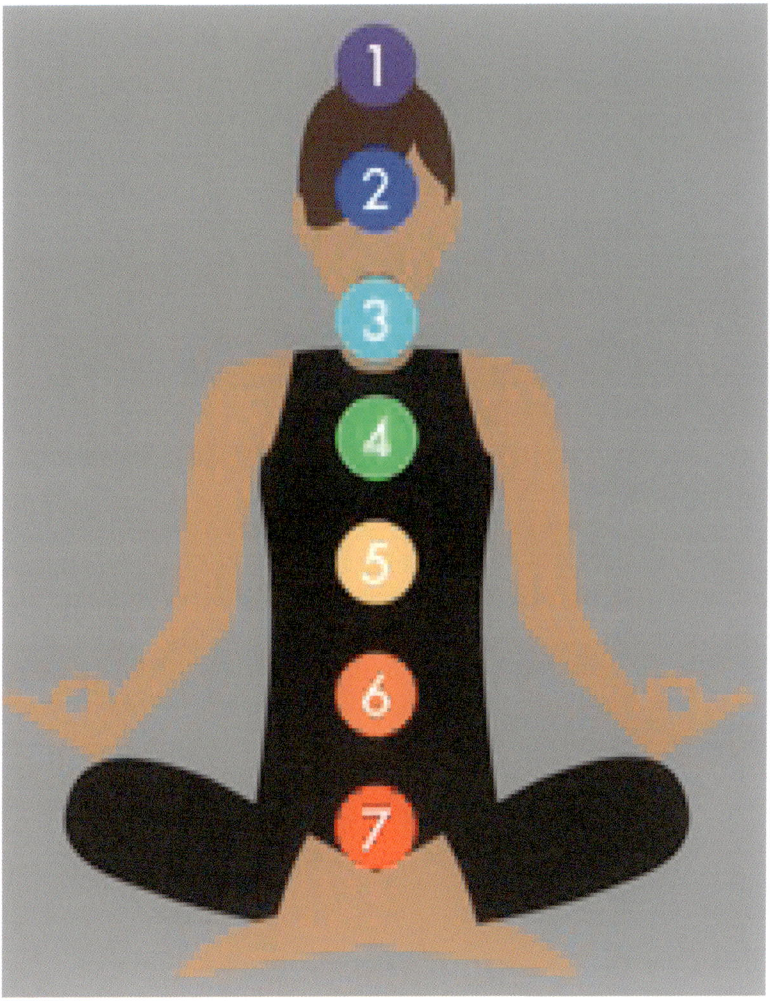
1
2
3
4
5
6
7

1. **Crown Chakra:** Universally connects us spiritually. Governs the brain, nervous system, and the pituitary gland. It is located at the top of the head and is violet in color.

2. **Third Eye Chakra:** Associated with our ability to rationalize, focus, and apply logic. Evokes inner wisdom as well as intuition and ESP (extrasensory perception). This chakra is connected to the pineal gland. It is in the forehead, above and between the eyes, and is indigo in color.

3. **Throat Chakra:** Responsible for communication and expressing personal truth and creativity. Associated with the mouth, thyroid gland, and endocrine system it is in the neck and throat and is blue in color.

4. **Heart Chakra:** Governs love and compassion and is associated with serenity and balance. Connected to the skin and hands. This chakra is in the center of the chest and is green in color.

5. **Solar Plexus Chakra:** Symbolizes intellect, ego, personality, and personal will. It is connected to the stomach, gall bladder, spleen, and liver. This chakra is in the stomach area and is yellow in color. Solar plexus chakra is one of the two core chakras.

6. **Sacral Chakra:** Responsible for sexuality, pleasure, emotion, creativity, and intimacy. This chakra is located just below the navel, in the lower abdomen, and is orange in color. The sacral chakra is one of the two core chakras.

7. **Root Chakra:** This chakra is associated with safety, survival as well as grounding to the earth. It is located at the base of the spine and is red in color.

Wealth...

Tamara cannot bring herself to clean her house. That is putting it mildly. The situation is well beyond some clutter and dust. Food litters her kitchen counter and dining room table. Clothes cover every inch of the floor. She feels stupid. Every time she looks around her home, she feels sad and ashamed.

She thinks of herself as a slob and basic loser. This, of course, depresses her further. But out in society, she is no slouch. We are talking about an independent woman managing a lucrative career. Publicly she has her act together, but privately, Tamara is suffering from what I call the "I CAN'T DO IT" (or ICDI) syndrome.

No one escapes the ICDI noose. It happens to all of us, in varying degrees. It is that inner dialogue that basically says, "I know I should do X, but I can't." It can apply to anything; work, relationships, diet, exercise, school or quitting an addiction.

To get Tamara out of her circle of negativity, I started her on a 3-week goal achievement plan. She also meditates to specifically strengthen her 3rd eye chakra. Week one consists of having Tamara concentrate on cleaning/organizing her bed and nightstand. She also must keep it clean. Week two involves tackling more areas of her house. And by week three, her entire home is free of debris.

Tamara is now able to find items quickly. She experiences better quality of sleep and she is more thoughtful about what she is eating. Her general health improves, but more importantly, she is no longer suffering from depression.

Reachable goals within a person's power are key. Depending on the situation and the person, the process can sometimes take up to a year to tackle. The person must possess a willingness to change one small thing at a time; to just do the next thing, if you will. As seen with Tamara, small milestones prevent her from feeling overwhelmed. Persistence coupled with baby steps enable a person to accomplish more and more as things progress. Suddenly tasks do not seem so difficult anymore. Consequently, more can be taken on with less effort.

Eliminating the physical debris allows Tamara to better focus on other areas of her life. Her 3rd eye chakra is now healthy and clear. She can find emotional wealth within her circle of friends and family. Confidently engaged in all aspects of life, she feels happy and satisfied.

Chapter 3: Crystals, The Throat Chakra & Energy

      Our planet is covered with abundances of energy. High concentrations of energy, flowing upward and inward, can be found more powerful near oceans and mountains. These high-density energy areas are known as vortexes.

      Famous for its beautiful red rock vistas, Sedona, Arizona is also known for its many vortexes. People from all over the world have journeyed to Sedona, reporting everything from tingling sensations and spiritual awakening to deeply sacred connections to the scarlet rock formations. These vortexes raise human vibration.

      In general terms, the Law of Vibration states that EVERYTHING, all matter, emits vibration; the dining room table, the grain of sand on the beach, the weeping willow along a country road, and even you. Your thoughts and feelings also have different vibrational energies or frequencies. High vibrational energy examples are feelings of gratitude, joy, and love. Low vibrational energy examples are feelings of fear, suffering and guilt.

Emotional Frequency Scale

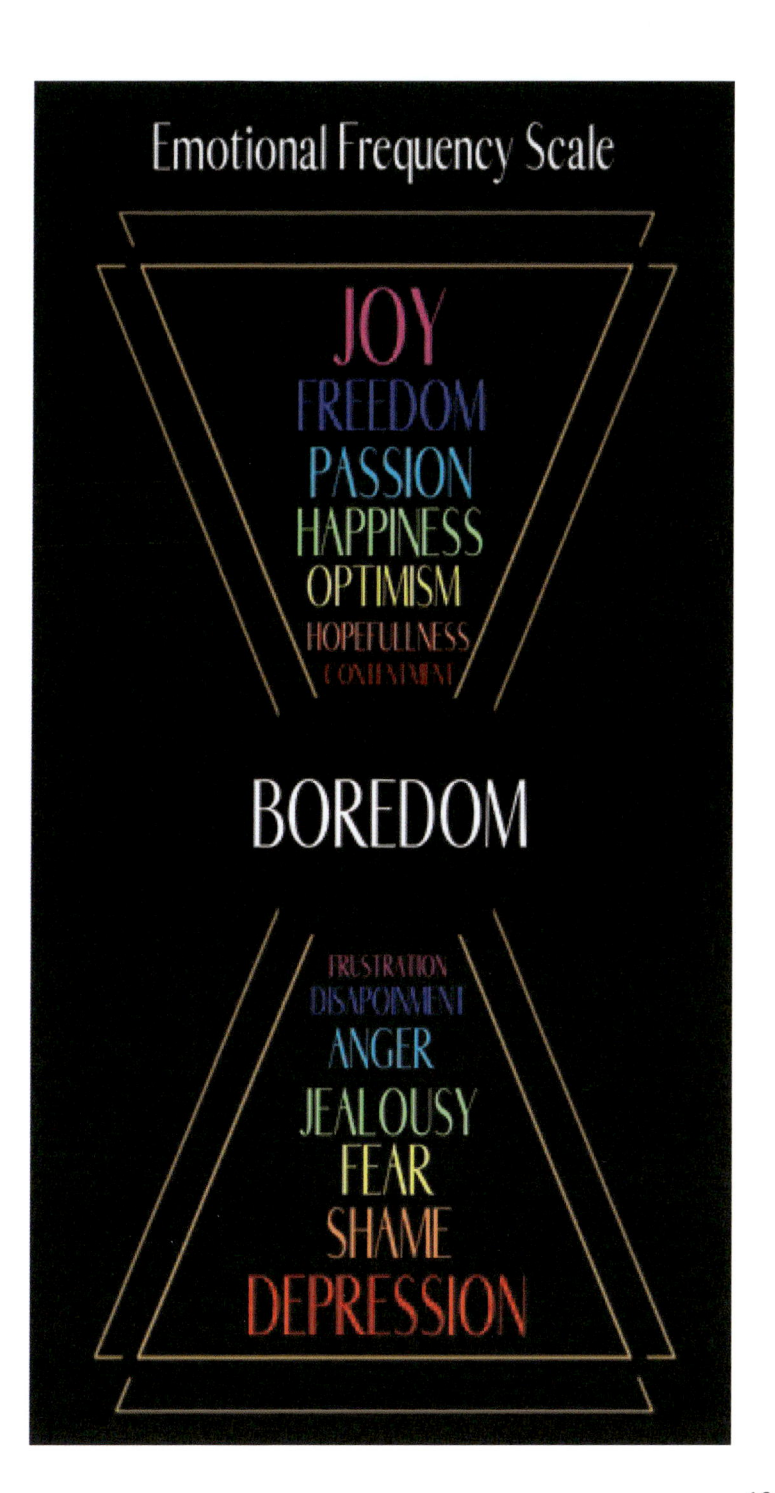

JOY
FREEDOM
PASSION
HAPPINESS
OPTIMISM
HOPEFULLNESS
CONTENTMENT

BOREDOM

FRUSTRATION
DISAPOINMENT
ANGER
JEALOUSY
FEAR
SHAME
DEPRESSION

Raising one's vibration to a high level is important so the low energy frequencies do not have a place to prosper. In other words, if you have strong feelings of bliss and appreciation, there is far less room for the low vibrational feelings to reside. If we have a high vibration, we attract good energy; we experience greater clarity, creativity, personal power, joy, and love. Conversely, if we have a low vibration, we attract negative energy. Your vibration dictates who and what you attract in your lifetime.

Crystals, like the rock formations of Sedona, are sources of high energy that have come from the largest collective crystal we know of Mother Earth. These semi-precious stones harness energy from the sun and moon, as well as our oceans. They possess powerful vibrations. Crystals allow positive, healing energy to flow into the body, thereby forcing out the negative energy.

Clear quartz, amethyst, and rose quartz aid in raising vibration. Clear quartz absorbs negative energy, bringing light to any darkness; cleaning and healing, eliminating toxins. Amethyst provides focus and clarity as well as helping to understand our individual purpose. Finally, rose quartz softens the heart; aiding in learning how to love yourself and others by sharing love healthily. These crystals play an integral part in establishing a higher vibration. An example of this is crystals healing our throat chakra, encouraging a person to speak their personal truth.

Rose Quartz, Amethyst & Clear Quartz

Energy…

  Teri likes numbers. She likes to count things. To her family, she is known for counting. She will report the number of railroad cars as she is waiting for a train to pass, or if she is working in the yard, she might count the number of pinecones collected.

  Five. That is the number of depressions Teri has endured over the course of 30 years. The shortest lasted 9 months and the longest continued for 22 months.

  When Teri and I met, she was not depressed. Due to her diplomatic and thoughtful nature, comments, and actions of others over the years had taken a tremendous toll emotionally. She blamed herself for feeling wounded – reasoning she was just "too sensitive."

  I only met with Teri three times in person. Through meditations with me, she became aware of the protective spiritual forces in her life. She began to feel safe. Before Teri flew home, I gave her a clear quartz crystal to hold while meditating.

  Holding that crystal in her hand brought comfort, feelings of serenity and completeness. Teri found the meditations therapeutic, to say the least. With every contemplation came empowerment. Soon her throat chakra was greatly strengthened.

  Expressing herself instilled feelings of confidence. She meditates daily with her crystal and looks forward to the relaxation. 4 years have passed with no depression in sight. Teri can speak her truth honestly and openly, and that has manifested in an energized, happy, satisfied lady.

Chapter 4: Essential Oils, The Heart Chakra & Love

Around the world, for thousands of years, many cultures have used essential oils for healing. These concentrated oils have been extracted from certain flowers, grasses, fruits, leaves, roots, and trees. Among countless beneficial properties, these oils have been frequently used to promote physical and emotional wellness.

Lavender, one of the most common essential oils, is known for its effective treatments of everything from burns to stimulating cells in wounds for quicker healing. Lavender is a natural antiseptic and antibiotic. It can aid with the psychological shock of injury. Lavender also plays an important role with the heart chakra. It calms strong emotions, causing relaxation, releasing stress and feelings of fear. Lavender helps to connect with the heart, thus opening to more love.

The Blue Mountains of New South Wales in Australia are named for the remarkable blue haze emitting from the resin of the eucalyptus gum trees. This haze is known to cover the landscape. In 1788, Eucalyptus was first distilled in Australia by two doctors, John White & Dennis Cossiden; their medical intention was to treat chest problems and colic. Today, it is often used as a decongestant to treat colds and bronchitis. Eucalyptus causes the chest area to open, encouraging energy flow through the heart chakra. This essential oil is known for calming and uplifting the spirit.

Documentation dating back to 1,000 B.C. shows that ancient cultures were fans of peppermint essential oil's versatile qualities. Its cooling effects relieve muscle pain, while the natural anti-inflammatory soothes the gastric lining and colon. Peppermint oil also assists with the calming and strengthening of the respiratory system. When emotions of rejection or jealousy occur, peppermint oil works to curtail tightening of the chest and eases shortness of breath; this is beneficial to the heart chakra in times of emotional turmoil.

Frequency of single essential oils	
Rose	320 MHz
Helichrysum	181 MHz
Frankincense	147 MHz
Ravensara	134 MHz
Lavender	118 MHz
German Chamomile	105 MHz
Idaho Tansy	105 MHz
Myrrh	105 MHz
Melissa	102 MHz
Juniper	98 MHz
Sandalwood	96 MHz
Angelica	85 MHz
Peppermint	78 MHz
Galbanum	56 MHz
Basil	52 MHz

Frequency of people and things	
Human Brain	72-90 MHz
Human Body (day)	62-68 MHz
Cold symptoms	58 MHz
Flu symptoms	57 MHz
Candida	55 MHz
Epstein-Barr	52 MHz
Cancer	42 MHz
Onset of death	25 MHz
Processed/canned food	0 MHz
Fresh produce	up to 15MHz
Dry herbs	12-22 MHz
Fresh herbs	20-27 MHz
Essential oils	52-320 MHz

Love...

I have a room devoted to meditation. Each client of mine has a specific crystal in this room, and I meditate for them using their personal crystal. Meditation provides me with a deeper understanding of what I need to be focusing on for each person. A client's energy appears to me in colors (usually light blue and gold), and that energy hovers above that person's crystal.

The following is my favorite story about love and divine intervention:

It was late in the evening when I got the call, which seemed strange for an initial reading. He said his name was Hugh and he needed immediate answers. Impressed with the information coming through in the reading, he continued to see me. Hugh's personal issues improved with each passing week. Through the process of strengthening his spirit-body-mind connection, we became friends.

A year after meeting Hugh, I met Holly. One of my clients suggested she call me –her readings would have to take place over the phone since Holly lived in Boston. Recently divorced, she was having difficulty processing it all; she did not understand why she was unable to make the marriage work. Holly became a client, and I began meditating for her.

During the meditations I noticed something odd – Holly's energy was moving closer to Hugh's energy. I thought this might be due to their crystals being too close, so I moved them further apart. But even with the added distance, her energy was still moving toward his. I continued to move the crystals. This went on for weeks.

Finally, after asking why this was happening, I received my answer. My job was to get Hugh and Holly to meet one another.

Without divulging any details, I explained to that for reasons unknown to me, there would need to be an introduction taking place on a conference call.

All I said was, "Hugh, meet Holly."

After about an hour of listening and saying absolutely nothing, I excused myself and hung up. They talked for hours. In fact, they spoke every day for months until they were finally able to meet in person. Hugh and Holly fell in love and eventually married. It has been ten years of bliss, and they are happier than they ever thought possible.

Chapter 5: Rooibos Tea, The Solar Plexus Chakra & Strength

Beginning with the Chinese, tea leaves have been added to water for thousands of years. Thanks to present day medical studies, the health benefits of tea have been proven.

During WWII, when it was virtually impossible to import tea from Asian countries, Rooibos tea (pronounced ROY-BOS) gained significant popularity. Since the Rooibos tea bush is found in a specific mountainous region of South Africa, this tea became an excellent substitute to Asian tea during those warring years.

More recently, after hundreds of studies on Rooibos tea, the advantages of drinking this tea are, in fact, numerous. In general, Rooibos' enzymes, chemical compounds and antioxidants reduce inflammation in the body while boosting the immune system. Some of the many Rooibos attributes include aiding digestion, lowering bad cholesterol, weight loss and the strengthening of bones. It is clear why this tea has become so widely popular.

Just as the Solar Plexus chakra is connected to confidence and self-esteem, Rooibos tea encourages internal strength.

Strength…

Something caused Sarina to look in my direction. I was helping a friend at a Holistic Health fair while my future client stood across from us, listening to a man talk about Himalayan salt lamps. When she turned and we made eye contact, she walked over to me. I was not working. I had no business cards with me. I had not planned on reading anyone. But within the span of a minute, I was shuffling my Tarot cards.

Later, after seeing Sarina two more times, I realized she was haunted by a significant amount of fear and it revolved around a snake phobia. Throughout her lifetime, she had an unbelievable amount of snake encounters, and although she was never attacked or bitten, her anxiety was rapidly increasing. Her quality of life was now affected. She was fearful every time she stepped outside.

With Sarina's permission, through meditation I was able to see into a past life where in fact she had been killed by a venomous snake. That past life experience followed her into this life. She then understood that there was an actual reason for the anxiety- that it was not some kind of mental weakness on her part.

We worked through it all, and after a few months she was able to better manage her fears. The anxiety had been limiting Sarina, but once it vanished, her strength emerged.

On a whim, she dropped by one day to hand deliver a Halloween invitation. As I read her creative use of words, I understood Sarina's purpose — to help and encourage people through writing. We discussed this and she agreed to script a specific project. Now she is inspired and motivated in an area she only dreamt about previously. Realizing her goals are attainable, she finds herself liberated, happy — and enthusiastically writing.

Chapter 6: Personalities, The Sacral Chakra & Health

For the last decade, I have noticed a common thread with my clients, a significant lack of internal connections. Often, people are not connected with God/Universe, other people, or themselves. I have also noticed less hugging, less shaking of hands, and less talking to our friends and loved ones. My theory is that our connections to our devices have significantly impacted our culture. I am not saying devices are bad. I happen to love my cellphone just as much as the next person, but there needs to be more of a balance - our internal connections need to be present.

Meditation reconnects. You do not have to look far to see how popular meditating has become. Even with our fast-paced, device-filled lives, introspection is emerging. Maybe this is a product of our technology-driven society. Whatever the reason, I passionately believe that taking time to quiet and focus the mind is imperative.

When I ask my clients to meditate, I consider their demeanors and daily schedules; this way I can tailor the meditation to the client. To provide a more customized meditation for the reader, I have correlated specific plans for the 4 different personalities according to The True Colors Personality Types (https://truecolorsintl.com/). People are grouped into color categories (gold, orange, blue and green).

Decide which color best describes your personality.

*GOLD:

Punctual, Organized, and Precise.

This personality needs structure and organization. Order, rules, respect, and dependability are important to a gold. Time is a key part of their life. They need to be on time and want others to be punctual as well. Following the plan or schedule is best for a gold personality.

Golds see themselves as:

-Efficient and Decisive
-Providing Security
-Firm
-Always Have a Point of View
-Realists
-Organized and Punctual
-Good Planners
-Good Time Managers

Others label them:

-Dull, Boring
-Stubborn
-Opinionated
-Judgmental
-Bossy
-Uptight
-Predictable
-Controlling

https://truecolorsintl.com/the-four-color-personalities/gold-personality-type/

*ORANGE:

Energetic, Spontaneous, Charming.

Challenges, excitement, and happiness come in the form of action. Oranges like creating a challenge so they can achieve a personal best. They become restless with structure and routine and are satisfied in careers that allow for independence and freedom.

Oranges see themselves as:

-Fun-Loving
-Spontaneous and Carefree
-Flexible and Adaptable
-Proficient and Capable
-Practical
-Problem Solvers
-Good Negotiators

Others label them:

-Irresponsible
-Flaky
-Goofs off too Much
-Disobeys Rules
-Manipulative
-Scattered
-Cluttered
-Uncontrollable
-Indecisive
-Not able to Stay on Task
-Not to be Trusted

https://truecolorsintl.com/the-four-color-personalities/orange-personality-type/

*BLUE:

Empathetic, Compassionate, Cooperative

Blues tend to need relationships and harmony. Genuine kindness, sincerity, and compassion are important. Harmony is a high need. When there is discord and upset, this personality will come in the form of a mediator and will try to fix the relationship in any way they can.

Blues see themselves as:

- Warm & Compassionate
- Romantic
- Spiritual and Idealistic
- Willing to Work Tirelessly for a Cause
- Unselfish and a Caretaker
- Empathetic & Affirming

Others label them:

- Overly Emotional
- Bleeding Hearts
- Hopelessly Naïve
- Easily Duped
- Weak
- Too Touchy-Feely
- Too Nice & Too Trusting
- Smothering

https://truecolorsintl.com/the-four-color-personalities/blue-personality-type

*GREEN:

Analytical, Intuitive, Visionary

This personality craves information. Data drives their soul and there is never enough data. In the workplace, green is an independent and conceptual thinker. They seek constant challenge. Building systems or developing models will satisfy the need for innovation.

Greens see themselves as:

-Powerful
-Creative and Visionary
-Original
-Eminently Reasonable
-Rational
-Calm, Not Emotional
-Precise, Not Repetitive

Others label them:

-Intellectual Snobs
-Not Caring About Others
-Unrealistic
-Eccentric or Weird
-Emotionally Controlled
-Cool
-Aloof
-Afraid to Open Up
-Critical and Fault Finding

https://truecolorsintl.com/the-four-color-personalities/green-personality-type/

Health…

> Steve, a micro engineer, called requesting an appointment with me. Immediately I could tell he was very bright but anti-social; connected to the virtual world instead of people, and full of mistrust. Maybe he was simply curious in general, or maybe he wanted to see whether I was a fraud- either way, from the moment he walked in the door, he was resistant.
>
> If someone is resistant when I am trying to tap in, their negative energy manifests in such a way that it is difficult for me to "see." With Steve, I could not see anything clearly; he was, in effect, blocking me. I explained to him that since he was not cooperating and being open during the process, it was a waste of time for me and a waste of money for him. When he became overtly rude, I asked him to leave.
>
> Intrigued that I refused to be paid for the abbreviated appointment, he called me the next day. He felt badly that no money had been exchanged and insisted on returning with a more open mind. During the second reading, he was not as guarded. His history of an early adoption surfaced, and he began to believe what I was seeing and saying. It was clear that Steve was disappointed in people. This was in addition to a feeling a general lack of trust toward everyone. He did not believe in love or a divine creator. He was altogether miserable.
>
> A year passes until Steve decides to contact me again. This time he is enlisting my help, hoping he can work through the issues that are keeping him from connecting to others. In turn, I give him action steps using meditation, tea, foot baths and crystals. Steve's sacral chakra would need to heal before he could learn how to

forgive people. He also needed to become less of a robot and begin giving people a chance in the trust department.

Steve's core chakras (solar plexus and sacral chakras) needed stimulation since there was no stimulation in this area whatsoever. With the core chakras lacking, connections with others were non-existent and his love life was greatly affected.

After several months of work, Steve was learning how to forgive- and he was beginning to trust. The same combination of meditations, crystals and oils do not work with every personality, so he found his customized routine beneficial and ultimately a success. It took some time, but eventually Steve learned to trust people. This trust, accompanied by his people connections, has allowed him to prosper. Happily, he is also in a positive and healthy relationship.

Chapter 7: The Process, The Root Chakra & Happiness

All color personalities will need the following items before beginning the process:

Crystals: 7 clear quartz
1 amethyst
1 rose quartz

Essential Oils: Specialized Chakra Essential Oil Blend (focused on your chosen chakra of work)

Tea: Rooibos Tea Blend (various options)

Foot Baths: Power & Success Mineral Salt Blend or Love & Passion Mineral Salt Blend

6-quart standard, plastic foot bath basin

Additionally, crystal & oil kits are available at Urban Meditation and online
www.urbanmeditationstudio.com

Gold

Heart, solar plexus, and sacral chakras need strengthening.

Set aside 30-60 minutes one day a week to meditate.

10-30 minutes of that time should be spent with feet in a soak bath with 7 clear quartz crystals in the water.

Amethyst should be held in the right hand while rose quartz should be held in the left hand.

Think about past and present feelings and situations you want to shed.

After foot soak, continue holding crystals in hands and imagine all the things you would like to have in your life.

Closing words to your meditation should involve saying "amen" "thank you" or "I have trust."

This closes open chakras, so you are not leaving yourself open to negative energy.

Foot soak oil combination:

Add 3 drops of Confidence or Intuition essential oil blend from Urban Meditation into footbath water.

Add 3 teaspoons Love & Passion Mineral Salt Blend

Shower Daily:

While showering, hold one of the crystals you feel connected to.

Tea:
Drink at least 1 cup of rooibos tea daily (hot or cold).

Orange

Crown, 3rd eye and root chakras need strengthening.

Since orange never has the time, there is no instructed meditation.

Instead, keep at least 3 crystals of choice in car, office, and purse/pocket.

When feeling the need to be centered or grounded, hold a crystal and ask for assistance.

Be sure to place crystals underneath bed or inside pillowcase to stay connected.

Try to afford 10 minutes for a foot soak one day a week.

Foot soak oil combination:

Add 7 drops of Focus or Power Essential Oil blends from Urban Meditation.

Add 3 quartz crystals to the water.

3 teaspoons of Power & Success Mineral Salt Blend

Tea:

Drink at least 1 cup of rooibos tea daily (hot or cold).

Blue

Crown, throat, and root chakras need strengthening.

Meditate twice a week, for 30 minutes, on back-to-back days.

Soak feet the first day with 7 clear quartz crystals in water, amethyst held in right hand and rose quartz held in left hand.

For 3-7 minutes, focus on pain and mistrust leaving you.

Afterward, think of all the positive people in your life, the places you love, and the things you want to accomplish. Think of the people you admire.

For the second day, place amethyst and rose quartz crystals on a chair and sit on top of them. Envision rooting to the earth like a tree.

Closing words to your meditations should involve saying "amen" or "Thank you. I have trust."

This closes open chakras, so you are not leaving yourself open to negative energy.

Foot soak oil combination:

Add 7 Voice or Power Essential Oil Blend from Urban Meditation

3 teaspoons Power & Success Mineral Salt Blend

Tea:

Drink at least 1 cup of rooibos tea daily (hot or cold).

Green

Crown, throat, and heart chakras need strengthening.

Greens like beautiful objects, so crystals in jewelry are beneficial to wear. Set a reminder 3 times a day to stop and think about how thankful you are to God/Universe for your gifts.

Have a screen saver image of something relaxing; a place you have been or a person you love.

Once a week, soak feet with clear quartz crystals in water, amethyst held in right hand and rose quartz held in left hand.

Think about past and present feelings and situations you want to shed.

Closing words to your meditations should involve saying "amen" or "Thank you. I have trust."

This closes open chakras, so you are not leaving yourself open to negative energy.

Foot soak oil combination:

Add 8 drops of Voice or Love essential oil blend from Urban Meditation.

3 teaspoons of Love & Passion Mineral Salt Blend

Tea:
Drink at least 1 cup of rooibos tea daily (hot or cold).

Happiness

Rachel was a successful and strong woman with a great career in sales. Everything seemed to be in place, working beautifully. She was happy with her success and was determined to continue developing her career.

And then the unexpected happened. Rachel fell deeply in love.

The relationship progressed, and over time they knew they wanted to spend their lives together. The only hiccup was that Rachel had to relocate. She winded up leaving her home, family and thriving business.

The arduous task of reestablishing herself professionally proved difficult and stressful. It did not take long before feelings of isolation and sadness took hold. Rachel found herself looking to her husband for the love and support she needed to get back to her former success. When that did not work, she came to me for a reading.

Together we began working on her root chakra, reestablishing self-knowledge, and grounding. Possessing a hard work ethic, Rachel felt as though she was deserving of the finer things in life, but deep down she felt unworthy. She needed to have her sense of power back, but to achieve that, she first needed to love herself.

Through meditation, and with the help of crystals and essential oils, she grew strong. Rachel began to make herself happy. Her power returned and that manifested in career success once again. Harmonization of her spirit and *physical body have brought about happiness and satisfaction in all areas of her life.*

Concluding Thoughts~

As human beings, no matter where we come from and regardless of our background, we share a common need to be happy. Happiness, sometimes seeming unreachable, is possible by following the plans. The goal is to be consistent enough to begin feeling better, stronger, and happier. Should you find yourself forgetting steps and feeling discouraged, simply return to your personality plans and begin moving forward again. Remember that satisfaction is within your reach.

Finally, I would like to acknowledge my clients who have enabled me to illustrate every chapter with personal experience; not only was it needed, but it is genuinely appreciated. I'll never forget your hope, strength, diligence, and faith.

Thank you,
Tanya

"Everything is **energy** and that's all there is to it. Match the **frequency** of the reality you want and you cannot help but get that reality."

-Albert Einstein

Printed in Great Britain
by Amazon